MORE DINOSAURS!

AND OTHER PREHISTORIC BEASTS

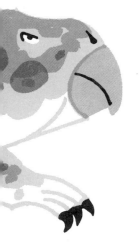

MORE DINOSAURS!

AND OTHER PREHISTORIC BEASTS

A DRAWING BOOK

BY

Michael Emberley

Little, Brown and Company
Boston   Toronto   London

First Paperback Edition

Library of Congress Cataloging-in-Publication Data

Emberley, Michael.
  More dinosaurs!

  Summary: Provides patterns for drawings of the
longisquama, protoceratops, woolly mammoth, and nine
other prehistoric animals, based on the evidence of
fossil remains.
ISBN 0-316-23424-9 (hc)
ISBN 0-316-23441-9 (pb)

83-9822

PB: 10 9 8 7 6 5 4 3 2 1

WOR

*Published simultaneously in Canada
by Little, Brown & Company (Canada) Limited*

PRINTED IN THE UNITED STATES OF AMERICA

CONTENTS

What, Where, How...

This row shows what to draw.

This row shows where to draw it.

All the animals in this book, no matter how complicated they seem, are made up of these simple, easy-to-draw shapes.

○ ▭ ▭ △ — ∩ ⌢

Each shape does not have to be drawn perfectly; you do not need a compass or a ruler. Slightly crooked lines will do just fine. 〰 means add color.

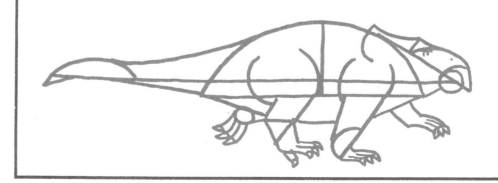

Protoceratops
(pro-to-SER-a-tops)
"early horned-face"
6 feet long

Etc.

Since no one has ever seen a living dinosaur, or any other prehistoric beast, you can color your drawings any way you want.

THIS IS THE ANIMAL'S NAME.
THIS IS HOW TO SAY IT.
THIS IS WHAT IT MEANS.
THIS IS HOW BIG IT WAS.

You can use the big pictures for coloring ideas, or you can just use your imagination. The drawings for this book were made with felt-tip pens; however, you can use pencil, crayon, paint, or anything else you have.

7

Longisquama

(long-is-QUA-ma)

"long scaled"

4 feet long

9

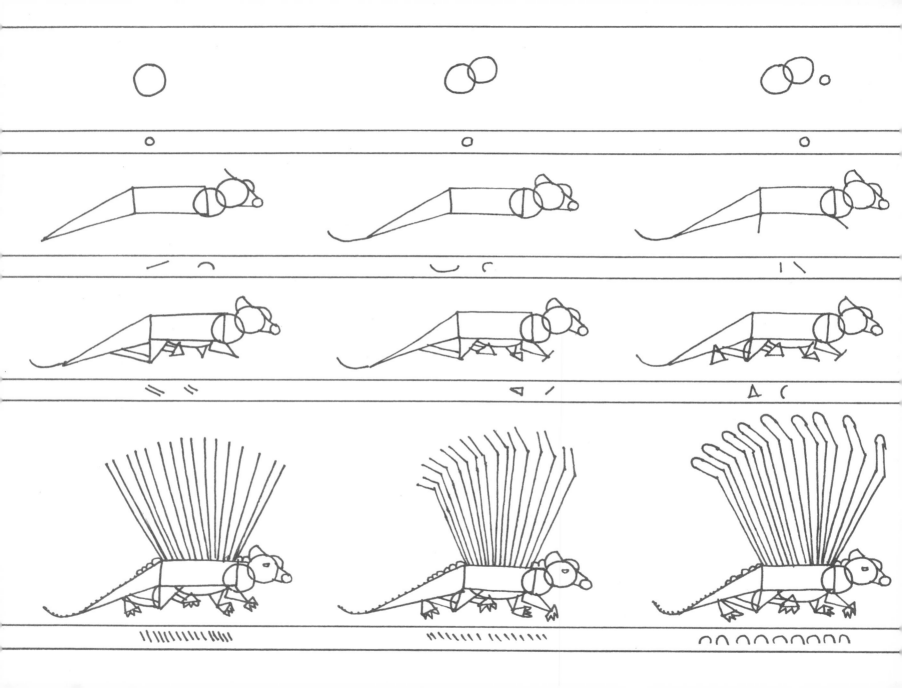

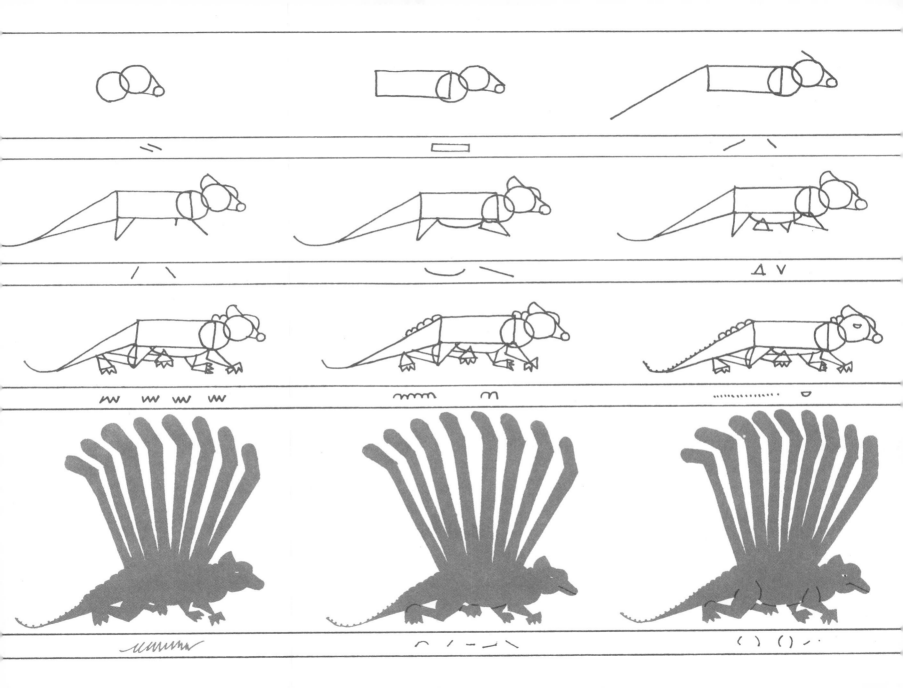

Protoceratops

(pro-to-SER-a-tops)
"early horned-face"
6 feet long

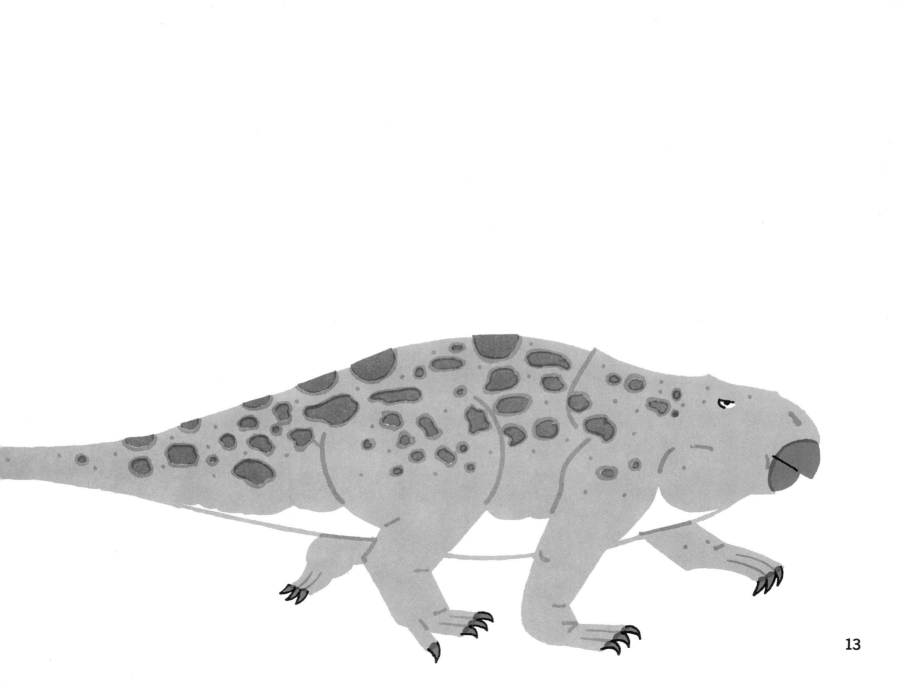

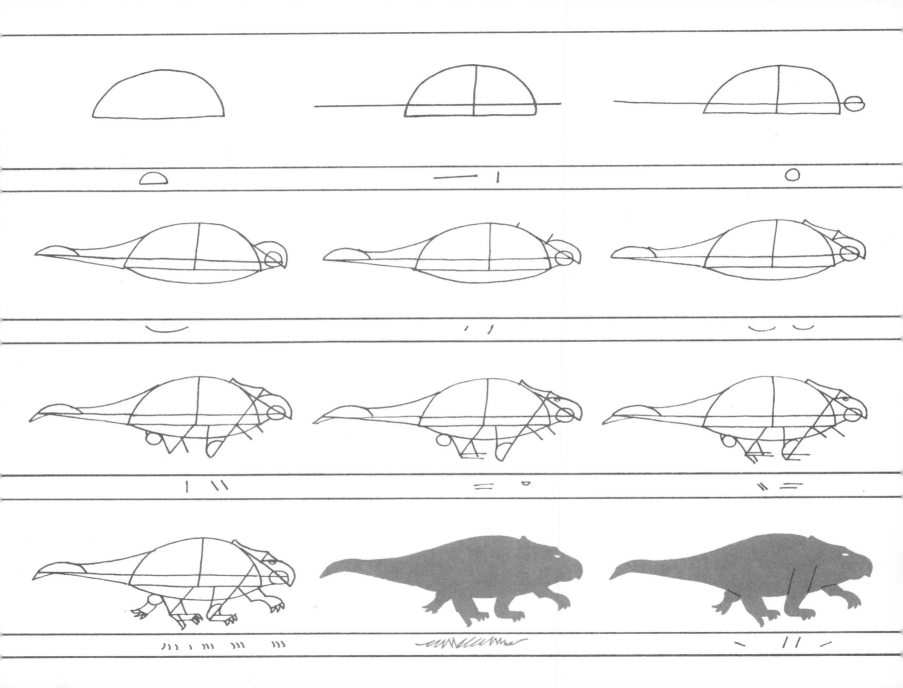

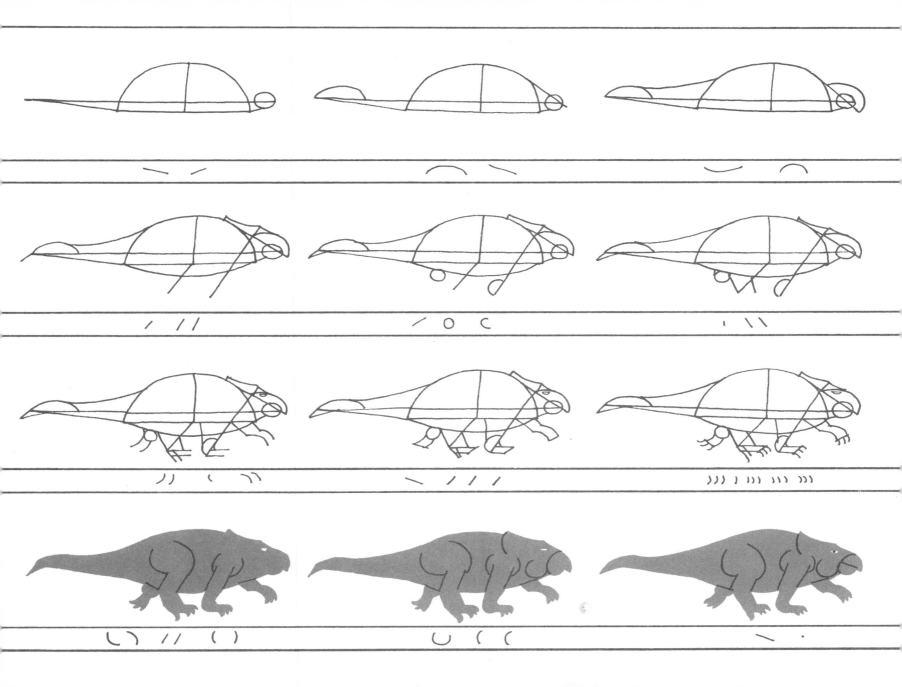

Dinichthys

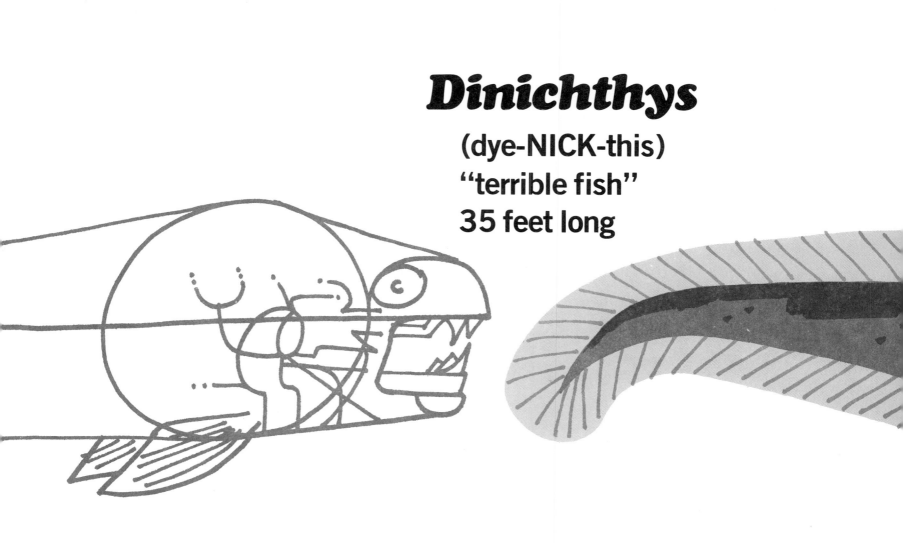

(dye-NICK-this)
"terrible fish"
35 feet long

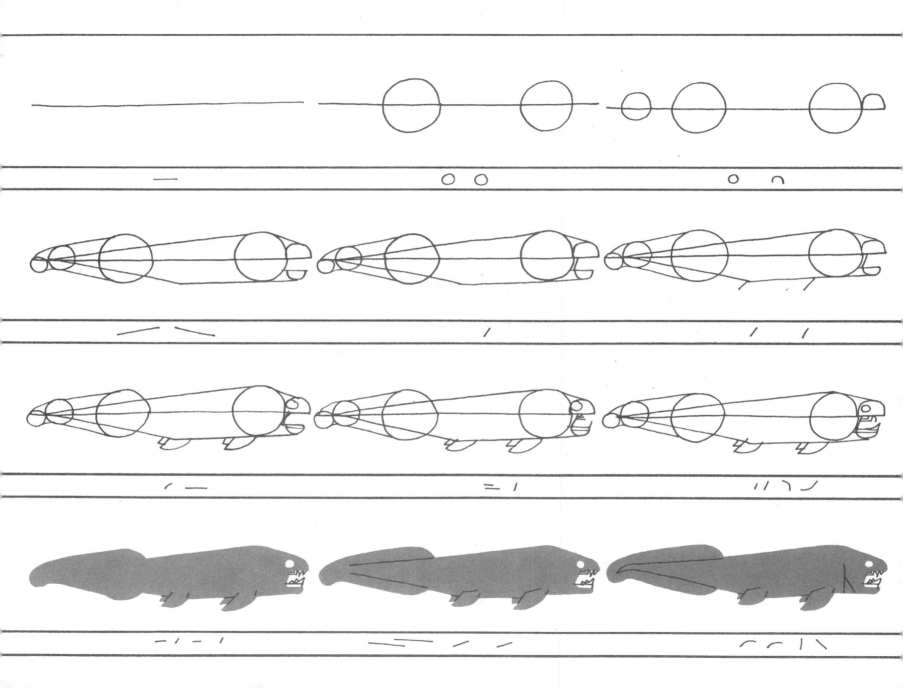

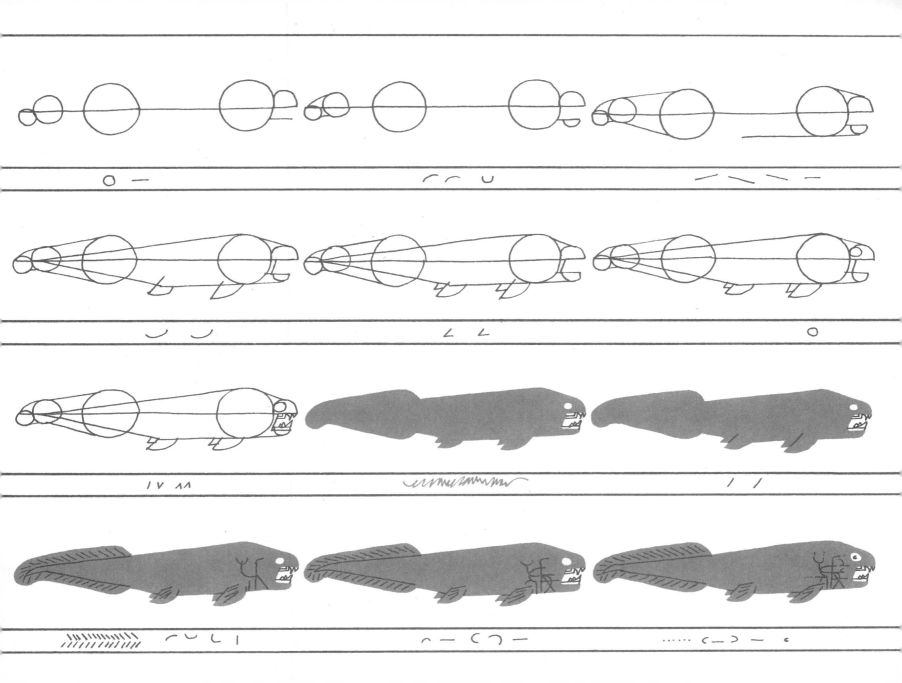

Dimorphodon

(dye-MOR-fo-don)
"two forms of teeth"
6-foot wingspan

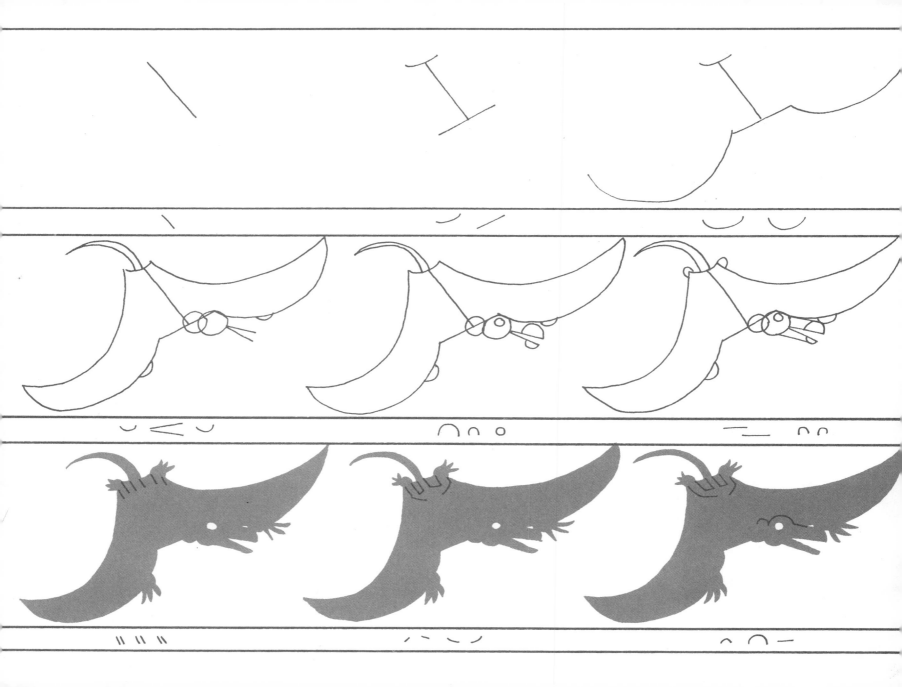

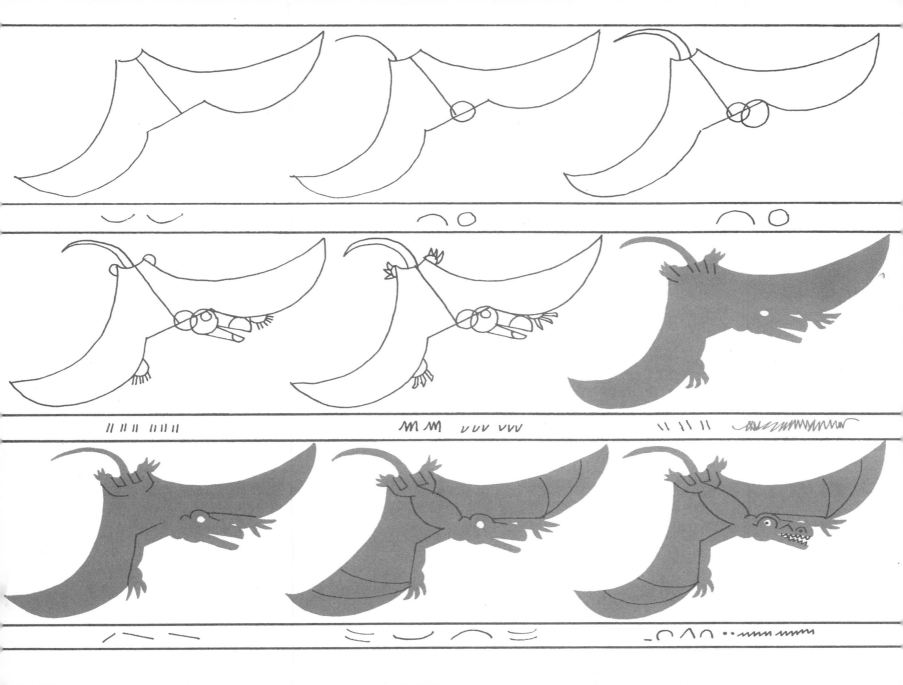

Ceratogaulus

(sair-a-to-GAW-lus)

"horned digger"

2 feet long

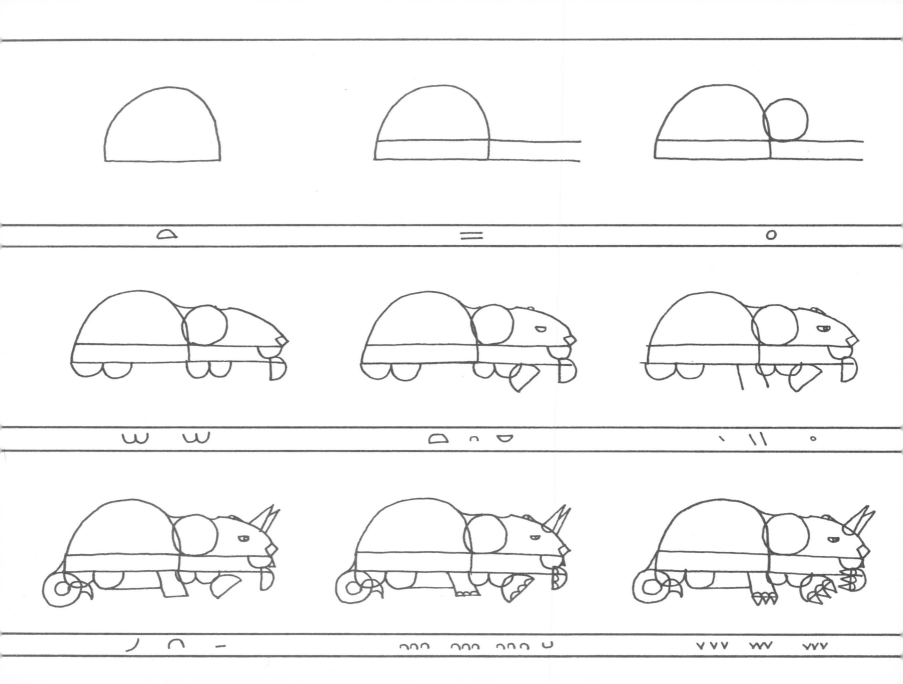

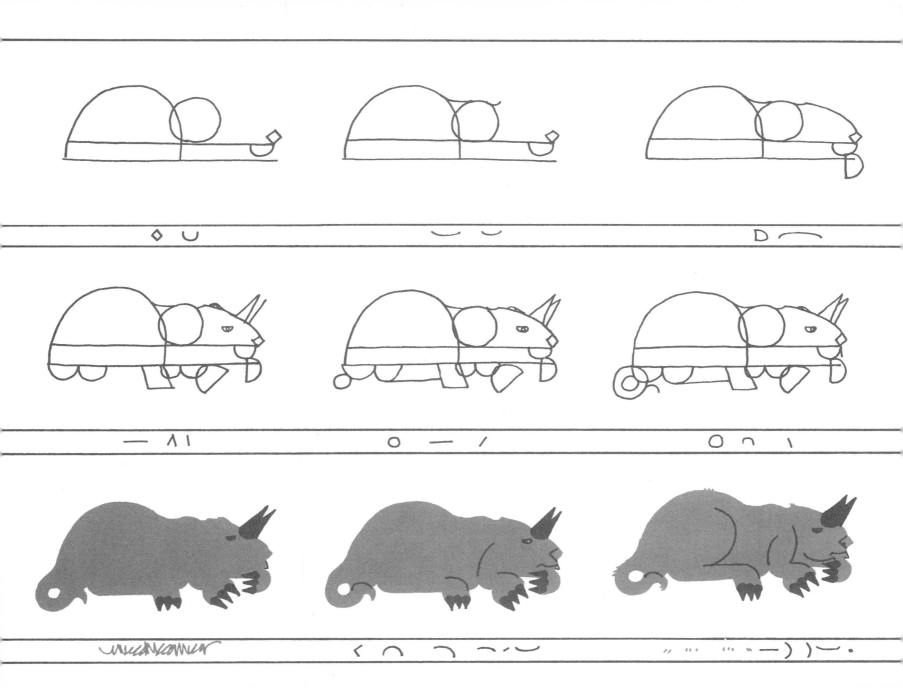

Zeuglodon

(ZOO-glow-don)
"strap tooth"
60 feet long

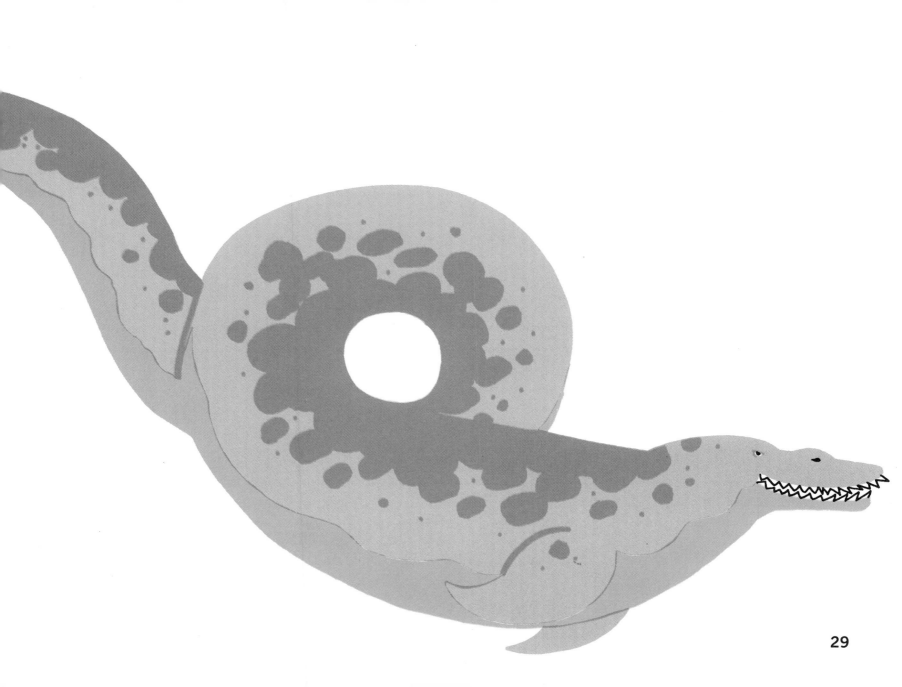

29

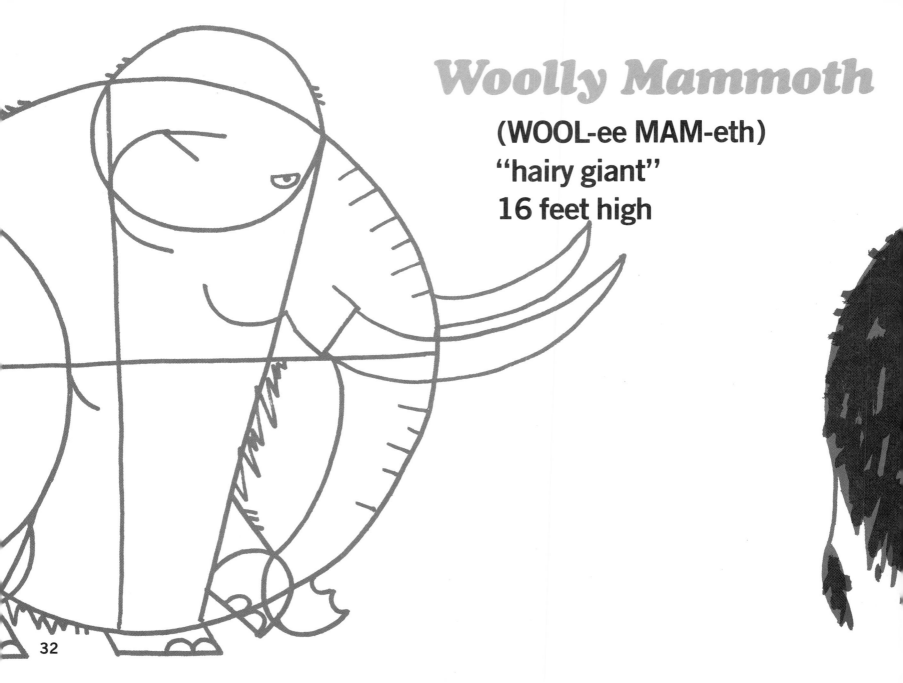

Woolly Mammoth

(WOOL-ee MAM-eth)
"hairy giant"
16 feet high

32

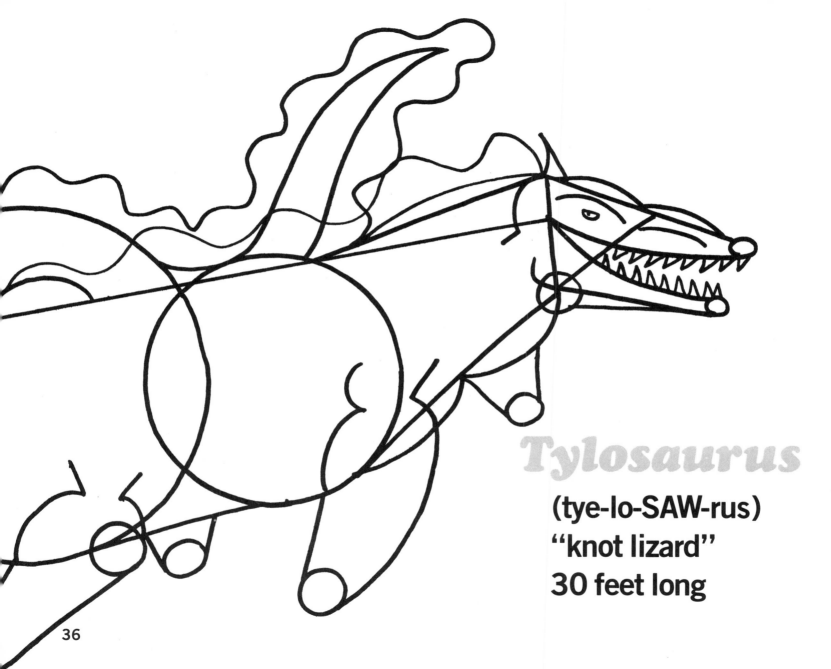

Tylosaurus
(tye-lo-SAW-rus)
"knot lizard"
30 feet long

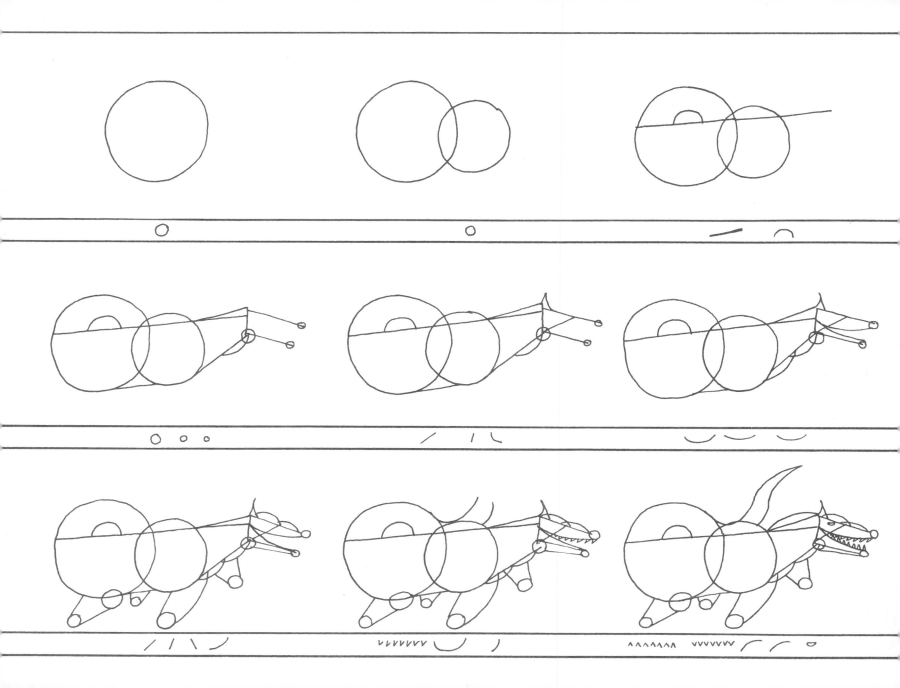

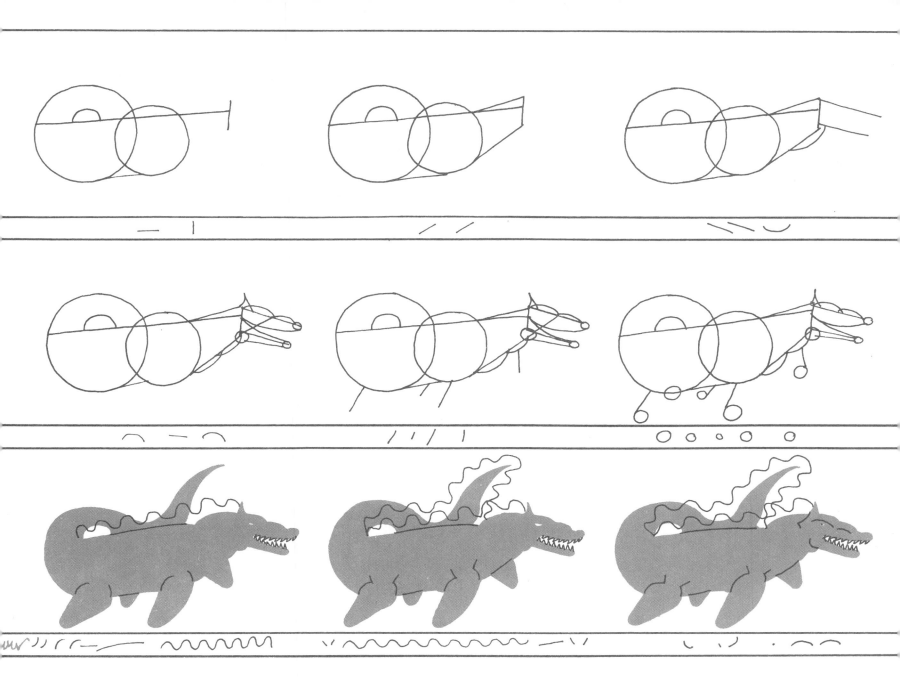

Glyptodont

(GLIP-to-dont)
"grooved tooth"
10 feet long

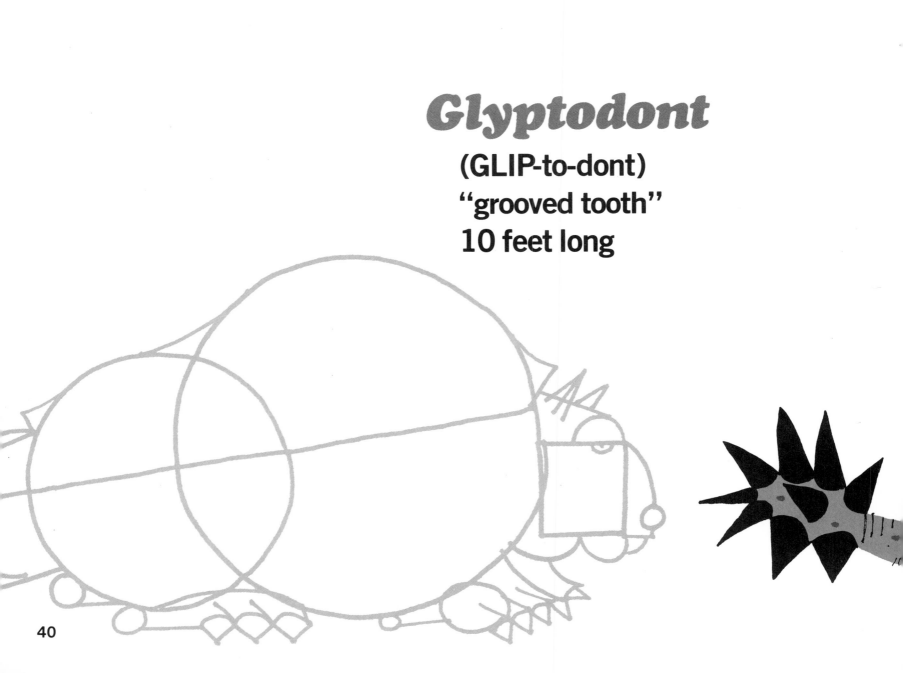

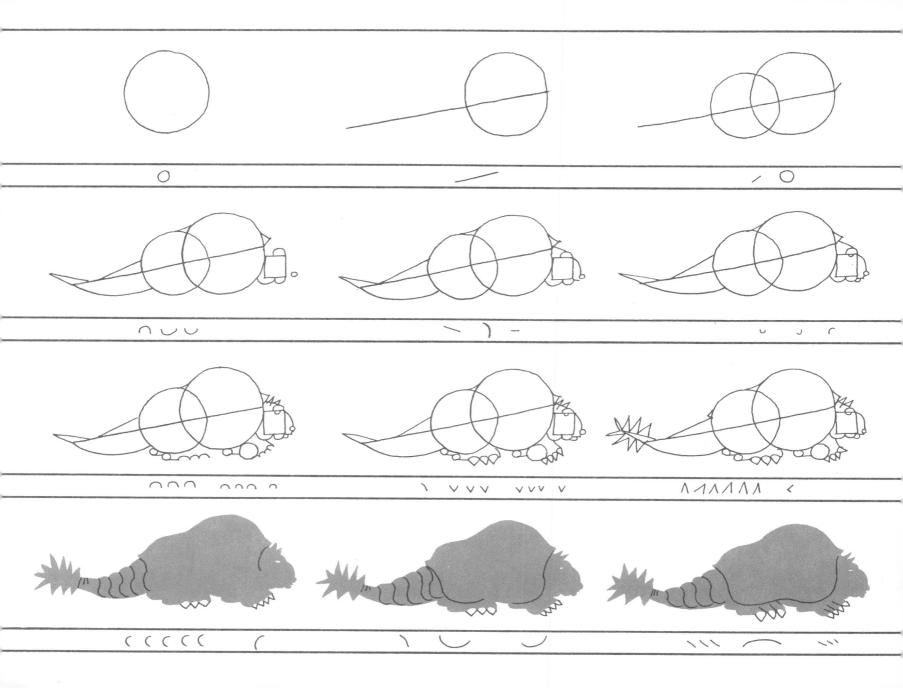

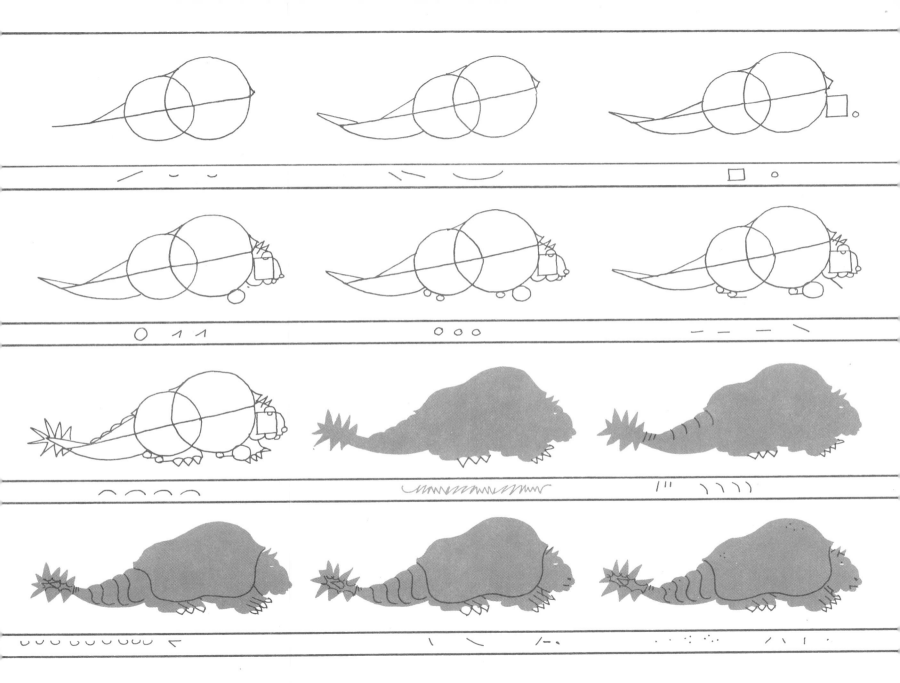

Archaeopteryx

(ar-key-OP-ter-icks)
"ancient wing"
18 inches long

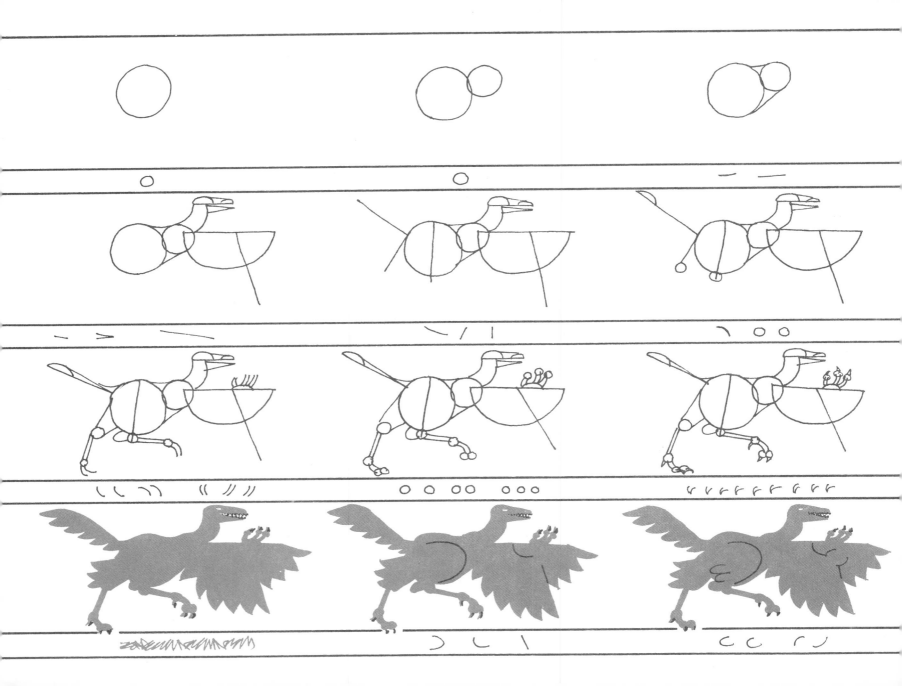

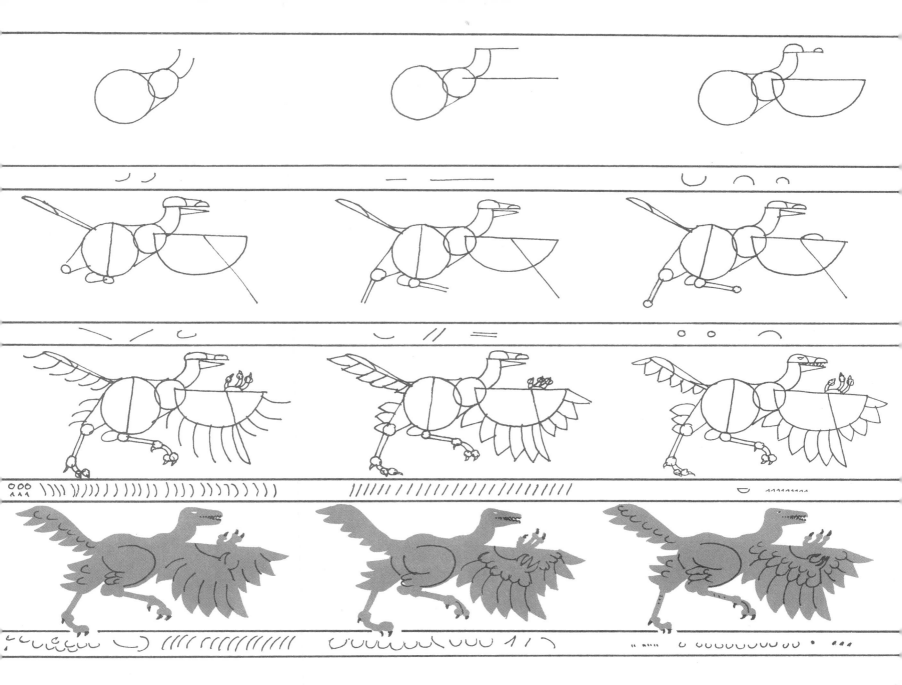

Smilodon

(SMILE-o-don)

"carving-knife tooth"

10 feet long

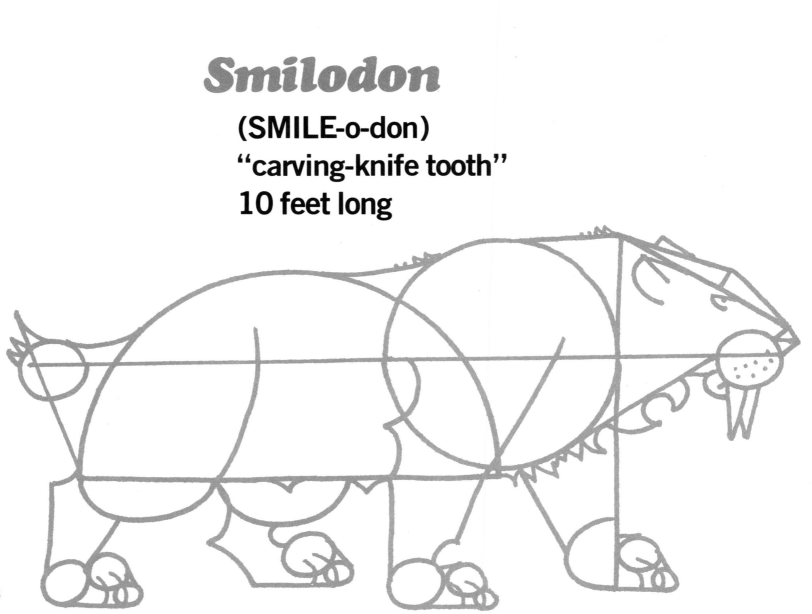

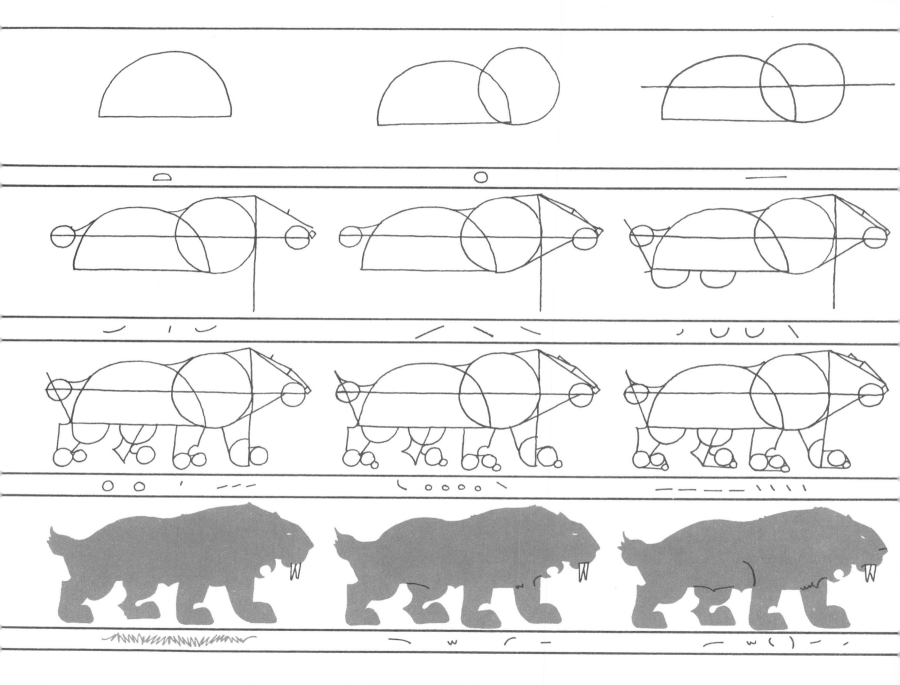

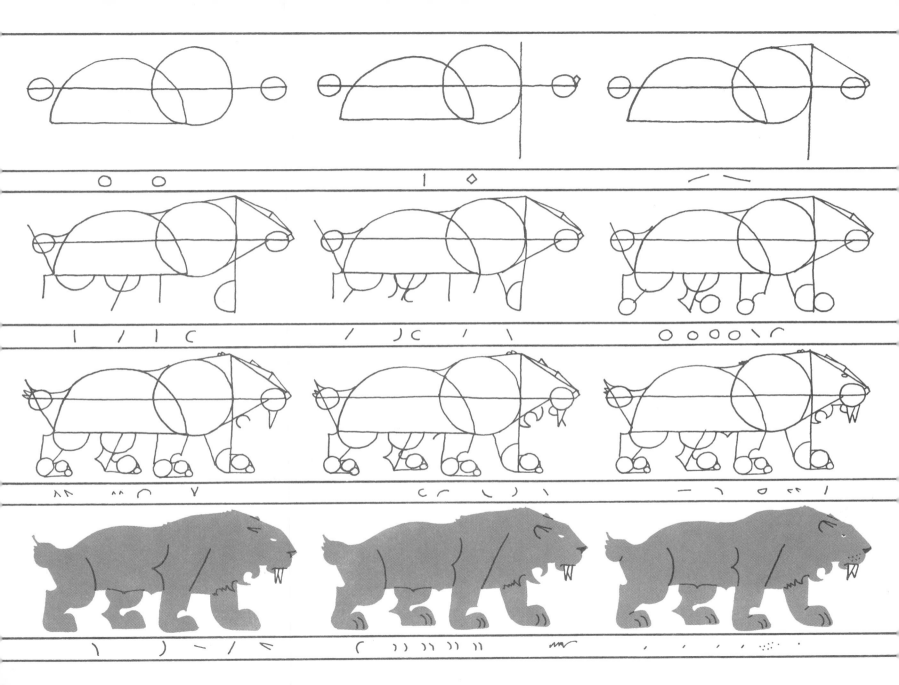

Baluchitherium

(bah-luke-i-THEE-ree-um)
"beast from Baluchistan"
18 feet high

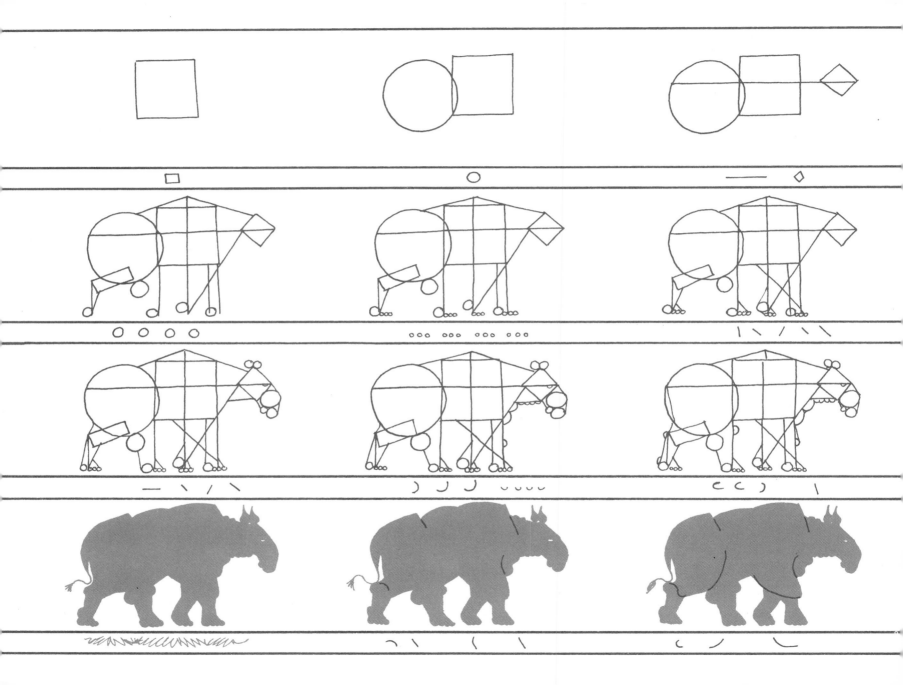

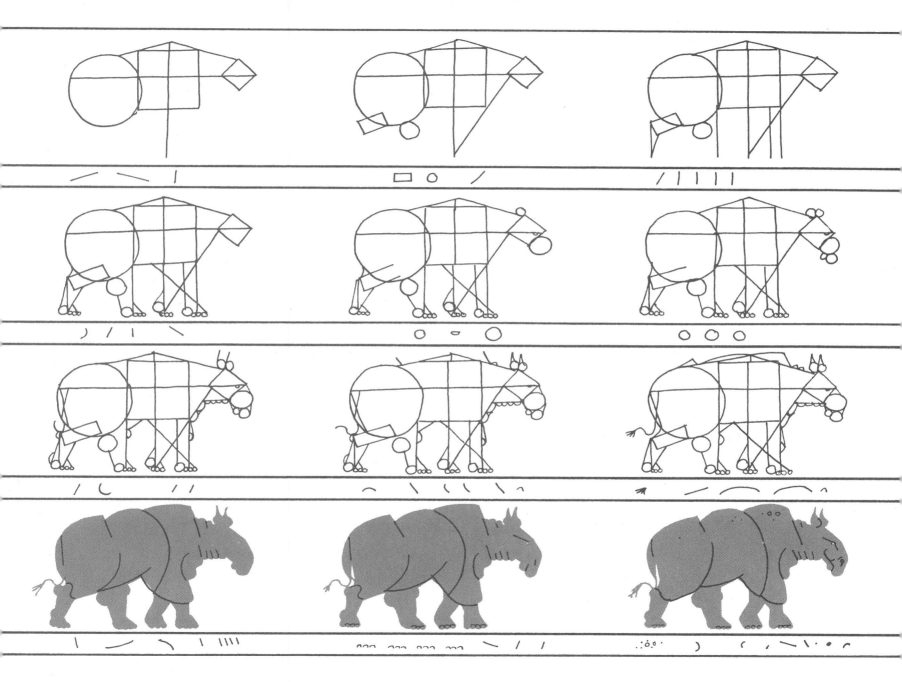

None of the animals in this book are alive today, but scientists can tell what they were like by studying the preserved impressions of their bones, which are called fossils. By comparing these fossils to the bones of living animals, scientists can get a good idea of what prehistoric animals looked like. Some of these animals have been easier to figure out than others. For instance, Zeuglodon bones were much like modern whale bones. Scientists were able to reconstruct the beast using what they have learned about whale anatomy.

Zeuglodon, Smilodon, Glyptodont, Baluchitherium, and Ceratogaulus are all mammals. They lived between 10 and 50 million years ago. The Woolly Mammoth is also a mammal, but it lived only 1 million years ago, about the time that another mammal, man, was beginning to emerge.

Protoceratops, Tylosaurus, Longisquama, and Dimorphodon are all reptile-like creatures that lived from 150 million years ago to about 70 million years ago, when this large group of creatures, known as the true dinosaurs, mysteriously died out. Archaeopteryx lived at the beginning of this time period; it was one of the earliest relatives of today's birds.

Last of all, the giant Dinichthys is a really ancient creature who was swimming the seas about the time that the first animals were crawling up on dry land, more than 350 million years ago!

This book's endsheets picture all the beasts together to show how their sizes would compare if they stood next to each other. They could not have posed for such a portrait, however, because they were never all alive at the same time.